When Grey Turns Blue

Poetic Reflections

by

Caroline Brae

Copyright © 2019 by Caroline Brae
ISBN 978-0-9978300-4-0
All rights reserved under International and Pan-American Conventions.
No parts of this book may be reproduced in any manner whatsoever without written permission from the author, except in the case of brief quotations embodied in critical articles and reviews.

Printed in the USA by National Media Services

Acknowledgements

I want to express my appreciation to those who encouraged me to step forward with a second book of poetic reflections including, but not limited to my family, friends, and poetry partners both near and far.

Much gratitude to Chris for his technical formatting savvy, which helped me fully realize my vision.

A special thank you to Mary Carnahan and the team at National Media Services, Inc. for their exceptional professionalism and service.

Much appreciation to R. Daniel Brown for sharing his inspiring photographs and for the resulting unique collaborations.

Ongoing gratitude for my poetic partnership with ARay, whose pen has diligently marked many a line in pursuit of excellence.

Editor: A. Ray Griffin

Cover Art, Design, and Photography, unless noted: Caroline Brae

Contact poet at Caroline.Brae@gmail.com or at Instagram.com/carolinebraebird

When Grey Turns Blue

Contents

Starting Over

Revisited	3
Falling	4
Gathering Moss	4
Shifting	4
Lingering On	5

Greyness

Cinders	9
Concealed	10
Fare Thee Well	11
Undone	12
Peri G	13

Turning

Unknown Graves-end	17
Be Gone	18
O'	19
Vate, No More	20
Margins	21

Footsteps

Unseen	25
Crossing the Line	26
Night Falling on Prospector's Hut	28
Dawn	30

Stepping Forward

    Heather Love   35

    Off Her Guard   36

    Her Story   38

    A Noble Path   40

    Remains   42

Blueness

    Tangent   45

    The Other Side   46

    Shadows   47

    Full   48

    Moonbeams   49

In Memory

    Memories   53

In memory of my Dad
who loved me unconditionally

and

Dedicated to my Mom
who shares with me her love of poetry and song

Starting Over

Revisited

Refocus, reclaim, redirect
Rewrite your story
Leave behind the chaos
That unsettled your soul
Go in search of Lady Bugs,
Dragon and fire - flies
Find the light
In your darkness

Falling

Traces of autumn
Leave their imprint
On the ground
Like departed souls
Leave their imprint
On our hearts

Gathering Moss

Frozen waters
Quietly nourish
Green growth
Waiting patiently
Beneath thick
Layers of ice
To transform
Unseen beauty
At spring thaw

Shifting

Nature teaches us to bend
So we do not break
Often heading in opposite
Directions than we started
Vertical turns horizontal
East becomes west
But a bend in the road
Does not break a tree

Lingering On

A familiar classic
Of the working man
A non-assuming
Straight forward
Hint of musk
With light-hearted
Touches of orange
And cinnamon
That distinctly
Remind me
Of you

Your last bottle
Sat on the bathroom counter
Right beside the Palmolive green aftershave
WORLD'S GREATEST FATHER
Trophy you kept for decades
Simply because your adoring daughter
Gave it to you as a present

I took the liberty of taking
Both remaining reminders
Home with me
Treasuring your sweet scent
Knowing each time I opened that bottle
I could sense your presence
And surround myself
With memories of you
If only for a passing
Heavenly sent moment
And smile

Greyness

Cinders

There were no bedtime stories
No fairy tales or nursery rhymes
No words to soften the worries
Of a little child's weary mind

No arms to tuck her in at night
Or whisper sweet dreams with a kiss
Only shadows dancing on the walls
Horrid visions, not night time bliss

There was only Cinderella
As told by Rogers & Hammerstein
Where lyrics told the story
A colorized film in nineteen sixty-five

Music she could remember, and so
She learned to sing nearly every song,
And dream, as she watched the dancers
At the Prince's ball glide gracefully along

And when she became frightened
Or sad upon life's way
She often would remember
The words she heard in refrain

In my own little corner
In my own little chair
I can be whatever
I want to be

Just as long as I stay in my own little corner
All alone in my own little chair

Concealed

Unwinding the coil
Of my tightly
Compartmentalized life, I found
A guarded imprisonment

Rules at every corner
Hidden below the surface
Rusty bars and palisades
Keeping me in my place

Invisible stakes
Tethering me
To preconceived notions
Holding me down

My feet unable
To carry me away
I remained - constrained
Until I grew wings

Fare Thee Well

Long before Miley
Conceived *Wrecking Ball*
Emmylou hit town
With her own siren call

No long neck bottles
Broken for a fight
No honky-tonk bar
On a Saturday night

No drinking, no dancing
Only hushed low light
In a concert hall
The fall of '95

A final encore
To close out the night
Brought Helter Skelter
With a blinding fright

Somehow the darkness
Released walled-up fears
Moved by haunting drums
And her piercing lyrics

I went the to river, but the river was dry
I fell to my knees, and I looked to the sky
I looked to the sky, and the spring rain fell
I saw the water from a deeper well

Tears streamed down
Pulse began to race
My heart swelled up
Demons on my face

I stared at my husband
My love, my life
I knew I'd no longer
Be his wife

Thought I'd died, and gone to hell
Looking for water in a deeper well

Undone

I juggle
A jumble
Of words
Floating in
And out
Of my head
Waiting
Wanting
For them
To settle
Into stillness
Until they create
Meaning
Upon my page
Unravel conflicts
Weighing down
My heart
Exhausting my spirit
Where there are no expressions
To release the pain
Of one and many
I begin again
To find my words
Despite my stumbling

Peri G

A sadness rose
Over the western mountains
As the Cold Moon
Beamed in golden tones
Rays reached down
Into the depths of my soul
Turning the tides
With an unimaginable force
Lifting my spirit
Out of my body
Leaving a vast space
Where my heart used to reside

Cresting the mountaintop
I stopped to pause
Overlooking the valley
Of my youthful dreams
And greatest fears
All one and the same
Dreams destroyed
Fears subsided, but
No point of return

Magically
That Super Moon
Appeared directly before me
As if shining strength
Back into the crevice
Where my heart waited
"Be patient my child"
It seemed to say
"Love will return"

Turning

Unknown Graves-end

She did not
Send an invitation
Across the ocean
To the wealthy
English gentlemen
To travel up tributaries
Of her homeland

                                          She did not ask
                                      For them to steal away
                            Virginity of her native-ness
                                Of her people and culture
                                    As they searched
                                    For gold and riches

She did not wish   To increase their power
To be molded or
Stuffed into clothes
Binding her playful spirit or
Converted to a religion
That denied sacred
Ancient beliefs

                                      She did not forsake
                                      Her earthly father
                                  When given as a token
                                  Of acceptance and peace
                              In marriage to a white man
                                    And transported
She did not want   To a distant world
To suffer a young death
In the bowels
Of a ship docked
In a foreign city
Far from home
And her heartbroken father

                                        She did not seek
                                          To be made
                                    A sexually charged
                                          Ambassador
                            Glorified as the young girl
                            Who saved a captain's life
She did not receive   And empowered a tobacco trade
Honor for her bravery
For her intelligence
For her sacrifice
For trying to build
A bridge of compromise

                     She simply wanted to go home

Be Gone

Oh, impetuous one
Relentless pursuit
Of ashes with hot coals
Wanting and needing
Needing and wanting
Not stopping to see
Your fire is burning
In un-welcomed territory
Leaping and bounding
Bounding and leaping
Out over the circle
Of sacred stones
Why oh why
Did you stop here?

O'

Oh, how she stands there so poised. Hand on hip, her elbow creating a perfect triangle with equal corners. She is a man-eater in a skintight dress with flared upward hand – perched as if waiting to be gifted from her next suitor or perhaps an unsuspecting fool.

Knee high boots built for kicking ass. They will catch your eye, but take you down in a heartbeat if you step out of line.

She is a wild one – the few, the proud to be – an honorary member of wild women everywhere.

She is a light, a beacon - calling in the lonely sailors at sea looking for loving arms. Her embrace a safe haven where they are held warm and tight, even if just for a night.

Perhaps, her sky-reaching palm is a question – if you please kind sir could you help me? Is she an angel in devil's clothes or a devil in disguise?

All the clichés you hear of women sighting them as evildoers – the ones to blame for a lover's demise.

Her hair is magic, flowing at will with the wind – reaching, always reaching towards the sky. Perhaps she'll find her wings there and fly away.

Vate, No More

She sits alone
In her life size
Dollhouse
A creation of love
Determination and hope

Her vision nearing
Completion – Yet
Small cracks remain
Not only in walls
But in her heart

Unable to patch up
Tiny fissures
Leaving her restless
From years of chaos
She ponders still

Quietly sipping her tea
She realizes the old song
Life is but a dream
Is indeed reality
Years float by quickly

Jumping from one star
To another – Wishing
Silently and out loud
Wishing endlessly
For dreams
To come true

Margins

I will not
Left justify
Use punctuation
Hinder my flow
Of self expression
To make you feel
More comfortable
I will
Center myself
On the page
As I attempt
To do so
In this chaos
Letting my words
Move organically
After years
Of constraint
Self imposed
From ongoing fear
Because I was beaten
Down, and down, and down
But I rise up
Centered, unconfined
And fly as a free bird

Footsteps

Unseen

A man walks by
With a loaf of bread
On his shoulder - its weight
Deceiving and heavy laden
For overused, worn out legs
Barely able to carry him
Much less an added burden
That few can see or fewer still
Would stop to ask if
He has need of anything else

His loaf of bread
Is his breakfast
Lunch and dinner
Meager funds
Make for lean times
This bread is his life
Not a remembrance
Of an entity who promises
To lighten his load
If only he would follow

They say…
Bread is life
Yet the man
Who walks by
With a loaf
Of Bread
On his shoulder
Is barely alive
Under the weight
Of his burdens

Crossing the Line

He was not in the habit
Of straddling both sides
Yet, he found himself
Standing in the middle
Of a divided yellow line

Photo by R. DANIEL BROWN

Here in the Valley of the Gods
He stopped without forewarning
And slowly turned around
To gaze out over the wondrous
Earthen sandstone sculptures

> Fixated first on Seven Sailors Butte
> He then eyed Battleship Rock
> And suddenly heard Elton's voice singing
> *Daniel is traveling tonight on a plane*
> *I can see the red tail lights heading to Spain*

Like many of his generation
He tried to escape that godforsaken
War, deemed conflict, and resulting trauma
He searched the clear blue desert sky
Only to hear – *I can see Daniel waving goodbye*

> He stood where Forrest Gump
> Calmly announced decades earlier
> *I'm pretty tired. Think I'll go home now.*
> *Mama always said, You've got to put the past*
> *Behind you, before you can move on*

Tom Hank's lines flowed freely from his lips
As Bernie's lyrics rang in his head
Transformed by their words, he remained
Perfectly still – centered in the road
Allowing grace to wash away his unseen dust

> It was here on Utah's US 163
> Between the likes of Arches National Park
> And Monument Valley his desperation faded
> No longer did his shadow block his view
> His face now warmed by the mid-day sun

Night Falling on Prospector's Hut

Night came on quickly
In the unforgiving desert
He had walked for miles
In search of respite
Not only from the scorching sun
But for his tired soul, Exhausted
From months of being on the road

                                          He was an East Coast man
                                        Not accustomed to sagebrush
                                    Sandstone arches or faded rattlers
                                    He had not known such intense heat
                                      Yet he found the rough terrain
                               Refreshing - here in wide open spaces
                                          He could breathe freely

Music from "High Noon" haunted him
Meandering incessantly and playing over
Repeatedly in his battered mind, Delirious
From the burning brightness surrounding him
He walked on without a destination
Simply trying to orient himself in a land
Where there are few permanent markers

                                      He stumbled upon an old hut
                                    Just as the sun was starting to set
                           Shadows appeared before his weary eyes
                             As shade had previously eluded him
                                He wondered out loud to himself
                             Was this place a cattle rancher's cabin?
                             Did an old miner make his fortune here?

Silvery wooden beams surprised him
So tightly laid, they kept position
Over an untold number of years
Yes, it was a secure hut
Surely having weathered many a storm
He hoped it would shelter him
Throughout the cold arid night

Twilight found his hand on two doorknobs
Twisting the simple devices tentatively at first
Not wanting to disturb what had survived for decades
He was not a thief or bandit
Or accustomed to helping himself to another's property
So he treated the old abode respectfully
As if it were his own home

He decided to try his luck through the back entrance
Somehow, its exterior frame was less warped
Perhaps from a less relenting angle of the sun
He pushed only three times against the sturdy door
Each time slightly increasing the weight of his body
On his shoulder, he leaned into this dark sanctuary

And told himself, *I will be safe here*

Photo by **R. DANIEL BROWN**

Dawn

Sunrise came in a blaze of glory
Filled with colors of the spectrum
Burning bright orange and yellow
Lifting into hues of violet and blue

A prodigy to some, an oddity to others
He had been invited to Santa Fe
And arrived with youthful enthusiasm
Accepting the unknown yellowcake

He was now aged, yet still strong
Of body, mind, and spirit
Stripped of his former life
He sought a place of peaceful refuge

The brilliance of this morning
Took him back to that fateful day
When he witnessed the culmination of
Working hidden away in a secluded desert

Little did he know that one day
He'd gladly exchange his hard earned
Black suit, white shirt, and tie for worn
Blue jeans, straw hat, and hiking boots

Losing his security clearance
Allowed him to change his identity
His face no longer recognizable
Beneath scruffy beard and greying hair

He had suffered a hard fate
Losing his son Daniel despite
Saving him from the draft and jungles
Of Vietnam by sending him to Spain

He replayed Oppenheimer's translated words
"Now, I am become death, the destroyer of worlds"
And understood him naming the bomb Trinity
He whispered to the morning sky these words

In nomine Patris, Filii, et Spiritus Sancti
He had come full circle

Photo by **R. DANIEL BROWN**

Stepping Forward

Heather Love

A sea of purple
For a violet rose
A color of compassion
Honoring untold woes

She thought her life was simple
She thought that she was plain
She spoke her mind with heartfelt tears
And the world will know her name

She stood for those who suffer
From unjust and unkind fates
She stood for those voices
Lost along the way

She thought her life was simple
She thought that she was plain
Until a day of violence
Thrust her into deadly fame

Her words of strong encouragement
Will cry around the world
And all those silent voices
Will no longer go unheard

For Heather's cry to others
In her love against mounting hate
Reminds us we should listen
And not to hesitate

Stand up for those downtrodden
Stand up for those beaten down
Stand up and love your brother
Let your eyes be colorblind

And when you are confronted
With bigotry and hate
Let Heather be your guiding light
May her death spark your flame

Off Her Guard

They swarmed like flies
Upon the sanctuary city
Where vineyards grow
Next to blue mountains
Much like the outlanders
Who descended upon the Ville
Of Charlotte's town the year prior

A quiet peaceful valley had soothed
Her weary soul following the violence
Not only upon local folks, but their town
Where in the end, one young woman
Heather Heyer
Lay dead among scores of horribly injured
In that godforsaken attack upon the unsuspecting

She kept vigil all year long
Returning to the place where Heather
Perished in one swift blow
By a _____ man who drove his car
Into a crowd of non-violent social protestors
Killing Heather instantly and wounding
Not only her friends and bystanders
But the town's very soul

And so she returned to the peaceful valley
To commemorate this year-long vigil
Of remembering, of gentle protesting
Of finding her social conscience
Once again among wilted flowers
Where handwritten messages
And chalk lined brick walls
Marked the street where Heather was slain

It was there she found her voice
Her vigil a slow melodious act
Placing poetic postcards in a sealed
Protective clear plastic envelope
Simply marked, "In Memory of Heather Heyer
Please take one for yourself and/or a friend"
365 days of dodging photographers
And reporters who descended upon
The Ville of Charlotte in search
Of answers to explain the day
That violence came to town

And so upon the one-year anniversary
Of Heather's death, her guard was down
And falsely thinking that the sole photographer
Noticeable to her usually observant eye had retreated
She stooped down one last time
To place a purple flower
And secure her messages of hope
Silently seeking closure on her vigil
To magnify Heather's voice

It was there - in that moment
Of losing herself and letting down her guard
He captured her essence
And she found herself
The face of mourning
For the Ville of Charlotte's town

Her Story

Her curves are gentle and graceful
Handiwork of Northeast artisans
From more than a hundred years ago
She traveled over multiple mountains
To arrive at her destination
An heirloom, a gift, a token of love
Encompassing the thoughtfulness of more than one

Delicate flowers scrolled in hand-carved panels
Simple, yet elegant in design
Deep, rich African mahogany
Rare and priceless in today's world
Unmeasurable in hers
She is a beloved albatross
Weighing half a ton and then some

Solid yet fragile - withstanding
Countless moves into untold rooms
Inhabiting entire walls or corners
Once she endured being turned vertical
Twisting unnaturally to avoid
Black wrought iron surrounding
An almost hidden entrance
To land in the most humble of abodes
Providing solace, joy, and inspiration
From the miles of heartache

Each slight touch of hand
Producing rich, deep tones
Matching her outer beauty
With her innermost musicality
Repeatedly noted as irreplaceable
By those tuning her strings
And marveling at the quality
Of her sound board

Wordless songs by classic masters
Bach's *Prelude* and Handel's *Saraband*
Ring out in close succession
Elton's *Your Song* and Neil's
I Am, I Said
With no one there
To listen

Her ivory and ebony keys
A constant reminder
Of my dear father and favorite aunt
An undying connection
With their unconditional love
Her story is my story
Our souls entwined

A Noble Path

Flashing green eyes
Dance beneath
Feathery golden strands
Of sun-kissed hair

A child of the mountains
She roamed back hills
Barefoot over coal filled
Mounds in a forgotten holler

Her story is unknown
Despite outward signs
Of a labored gait
Southern swing step

Her pride as strong
As the metal crutch
And pieces of steel
Embedded in leg and hip

Pure determination
Kept her from dying
Saving her bleached kerosene
Soaked mother from being torched

Faint memories
Of witnessing her sister
Mysteriously slip
Into permanent sleep

One fiery spirit
Standing up against
Alcohol fueled rage
Three times her size

Tiny hands no match
For an ugly monster
Hurling her small body
Like a rag doll

No one there
To hear the sound
Of her crashing
Against a wooden planked wall

Growing bones smashed
Permanently dislodged
Yet she ran barefoot
Into snow covered hills

Willful beyond measure
Pure grit and faith
Kept her alive
Enduring pain filled misery

She keeps her distance still
Armed with memories
That moments matter
When in harm's way

Instinctively knowing
Love hurts
She replaces hugs
With warm smiles

Weary green eyes
Dance beneath
Feathery silver strands
Of sun-kissed hair

Remains

An alley of Live Oaks
Adorned in dangling Spanish moss
Did not welcome most folks
With a mint julep in hand

                                        Horse drawn carriages
                                            With seats of velvet
                                       And hand-carved wood
                                       Did not ease burdened
                                 Journeys over high mountains
                                       Or through low valleys

Where men and women
Worked with their backs
Laboring in unsafe
Mines and factories

                              Struggling through daily chores
                        Without running water or electricity
                                Working themselves senseless
                                    Until they turned shades
                                    Of grey from exhaustion

Moonshine, brew, and cheap whiskey
Eased their pain while
Cigarettes calmed shaking hands
As they quietly discussed
World events they could not change
But that changed their lives forever

                                       The Old South is alive
                                         But it is not well
                                   Still filled with poverty
                                   Where hard liquor
                                   Turned to hard drugs
                                   Meth filling the place
                                Of suffocating Black Lung

Aspirations dimmed
By the unsettled coal dust
Replacing uncertainty
Of the next day or hour
With desperation

                                  Perhaps slow, thoughtful
                                  Gentle natures could not
                               Withstand the changing winds
                                 That erased all they knew
                                  The Old South is alive
                                      But it is not well

Blueness

Tangent

He built a light-filled sanctuary
To join his soul with a cornfield
Planting roses, flowers, and trees
Attracting birds of many feathers
Flocking together at his back doorstep

He sits in silence often times
Gazing out over the crops
Rotating to soy every other year
Blue Ridge Mountains a quiet backdrop
To the sounds of a frequently used railroad

He is at peace in his abode
Though late in coming
It is his home and workshop
Where he designs and weaves
Works of art he will not sell

His creations are an expression
Of labyrinths he has traversed
Sometimes to faraway corners
Or more closely entwined
To horrors no one should endure

His mind filled with knowledge
Of this world and unknown galaxies
Language that only a few can understand
Brilliant and wise, he will alarm you
Speaking aloud closely held truths

His generosity apparent in his hospitality
Sharing assorted fresh fruits and cheese
With an old friend who he remembers
Dislikes sandwiches and coffee, preferring hot tea
Knowing he sees her, she walks away stunned

The Other Side

It is a dark place
On the other side
Of your scars
It is where you hide
Your shame and confusion
Compounded by guilt
From all you did not
Understand or stop

The Dark Side
Is not illuminated
By the light
Of the moon
Searching for Pink
In Floyd's seemingly
Never ending void
You feel lost

Unable to break free
Or much less *break*
On through to the other side
You become paralyzed
By your past
And your secrets
Which you struggle
To keep hidden

Yet, you still hear
The Doors screaming
"Try to run, try to hide
She get high, she get high"
Only to return
To Floyd's void
Of scars you can't hide

            It is there
          In the utter darkness
         You hear the uncertain
        Pounding riff you thought
       A mighty Hammond organ
      Only to discover Vox Continental
      Lightening your load, and you
        Arrive on the other side

Shadows

She sits and stares
At shadows dancing
Across her wall
Wondering how
The light
Ever reached her
At all

Full

When I could not find my words…
                                        I danced

When my heart overflowed with grief…
                                          I heard music

When I had nowhere else to go…
                                          I sat in silence

Until my words found me…

I wrote until the jumbled pieces
Pieced themselves together
Slowly with jagged edges
Rough and scattered
Piercing and exhausting
Until I felt there was nothing
More I could say or do

I filled your void…
                                          With my words

I filled your void…
                                          With my music

I filled your void…
                                          With my movement

Your love still lives on…
                                          Quietly and softly warming my heart

Moonbeams

"Unpack and release your weariness," he said.
"Unbridle me," she whispered softly to him,
"So I too can jump over the moon."

Nietzsche warned, *if you gaze into the abyss*
The abyss will also gaze into you
Thus Spoke Zarathustra

Per amica silentia lunae
Yeats quietly whispered
Bella luna – why make me wait?
Have I hidden in the dark for so long
That I cannot rise from the bottomless pit
To shine my light amidst the moonbeams
Burn brightly like the brilliant stars
Light years away, yet seemingly
At my fingertips reaching into the night sky?

I have touched the dark side
And know as Newton, *for every action, there is*
An equal and opposite reaction

Her whisper suddenly turned into a roar
Vibrating the lasso that suspended her
Dangling in the black night
And her voice began to echo
To the far reaches of the universe
Connecting with the expansive sound of a-um
Where moonbeams ushered her into the dawn
Until she was fully surrounded by light
Realizing her lasso had disappeared
She was free to move at Will
Between the dark and the light

In Memory

Memories

You sat at this table through winter and spring,
fitting together the pieces of your last puzzle.
Unable to sit here in summer,
you passed with the coming of autumn.
Miss you every season - every moment Dad -
but your light continues to shine.

About the Poet

Caroline Brae hails from the mountains of central Virginia. A former teacher, she has recently enjoyed creating workshops on developing a chapbook, writing poetry as an expression of grief, as well as hosting a fall writing retreat on finding inspiration in unexpected places. She has continued her explorations in the performing arts with choreography to her poetry and music, as well as sharing her musical compositions on both piano and autoharp. Works from her first poetic endeavor *Little Grey Bird* can be found at vox poetica online, The Sock Poetry Series at WINLifeTV, and on Instagram @carolinebraebird where she combines her poetry and photography. She is grateful beyond words for her local and global connections, and for each person who has enriched her life.

Printed in the USA
ISBN 978-0-9978300-4-0